THE
Archive Photographs
SERIES
SUNDERLAND AFC
1879-1973

THE
Archive Photographs
SERIES

SUNDERLAND AFC
1879-1973

Compiled by
Alan Brett and George Hoare

CHALFORD

First published 1996
Copyright © Alan Brett and George Hoare, 1996

The Chalford Publishing Company
St Mary's Mill, Chalford,
Stroud, Gloucestershire, GL6 8NX

ISBN 0 7524 0716 3

Typesetting and origination by
The Chalford Publishing Company
Printed in Great Britain by
Redwood Books, Trowbridge

Acknowledgements

The Authors would like to thank the following individuals and organisations for their help with this publication.

Stuart Bell, Thomas Carney, Keith Charlton, Phil Curtis, *Daily Express*, David Dodds, *Evening Standard*, *Football Echo*, George Forster, Peter Gibson, Phil Hall, Harry Langton, *London Illustrated News*, Monkwearmouth Library, Alex Murray, *Newcastle Chronicle & Journal*, *Northeast Press*, Pat O'Brien, *Shields Gazette*, *Sunday Pictorial*, Sunderland Central Library, *Sunderland Echo*, Sunderland Supporters' Association, *Weekly Courier*, *Weekly Illustrated*.

Special thanks to Andrew Clark, North East Editor of Chalford Publishing.

Bibliography

Raich Carter, *Footballer's Progress*, Sporting Handbooks 1950
Charles Buchan, *A Lifetime in Football*, Phoenix House 1950
Alfred Gibson & William Pickford, *Association Football & The Men Who Made It*, Caxton 1906
Simon Inglis, *Football Grounds of England and Wales*, Collins 1983
Simon Inglis, *Soccer in the Dock*, Collins 1985
Len Shackleton, *Clown Prince of Soccer*, Nicholas Kaye 1955
Alan Brett & Andrew Clark, *Sunderland Annuals 1990 – 1996*, Black Cat Publications
Alan Brett & Andrew Clark, *Newcastle United v Sunderland*, Black Cat Publications 1995

Contents

Blackpool goalkeeper George Farm in action at Roker Park. In the late 1940s and early '50s the star-studded Blackpool side containing the likes of Stanley Matthews and Stan Mortensen were one of the biggest attractions in the game. On 12 April 1948 the Seasiders drew a record League attendance to Roker Park of 61,084. New figures were again set by Blackpool's visit the following season with 64,889 packing the ground.

Introduction

This unique collection of photographs and memorabilia was amassed over a half a century and illustrates Sunderland's remarkable history. Formed in 1879 by a group of local schoolteachers, after opening its doors to outsiders the club never looked back. Even before entering the Football League, Sunderland already had an outstanding side and were known as the 'Team of All the Talents.'

Having first played on the Blue House Field the club made several moves in the early years. These included Groves Field, Horatio Street and Abbs Field before settling at Newcastle Road. From September 1890 Sunderland lost only one home game in the next six years. With Scottish stars like Ted Doig, Johnny Campbell and Hugh Wilson Sunderland won three championship during this period.

After moving to Roker Park in 1898 success continued and a fourth championship was won. This period before the First World War was another golden era for the club. Its most famous victory came on 5 December 1908 when deadly rivals Newcastle United were thrashed 9-1 at St James' Park. In the 1912-13 season the League and Cup 'Double' was almost achieved but a 1-0 defeat by Aston Villa before a 120,000 crowd at Crystal Palace ended this dream.

Sunderland's FA Cup jinx was to last almost a quarter of century until Hendon-born Raich Carter became the first Roker skipper to lift the famous trophy. This outstanding side had claimed Sunderland's sixth championship trophy the previous season. At this time Sunderland drew record crowds around the country and this continued after the Second World War when they were named the 'Bank of England Club'. Their big spending in the transfer market failed to bring further honours to Roker Park. The closest they came to a further League title came in the 1949-50 season. A freak defeat at the hands of bottom of the table Manchester City at Roker Park cost Sunderland the championship. During this season the aggregate attendance topped the one million mark for the first time.

Sunderland's proud record of only having played in the top division came to an end in 1958 when the club suffered its first ever relegation. After coming heartbreakingly close to promotion on a number of occasions a return to the top flight was finally achieved under the leadership of 'Player of the Century' Charlie Hurley.

By the end of the decade Sunderland were again relegated and the club's fortunes were at one of the lowest points in its history. The appointment of Bob Stokoe was to inspire a revival. The fairy tale success at Wembley brought Sunderland back to the centre of the world stage.

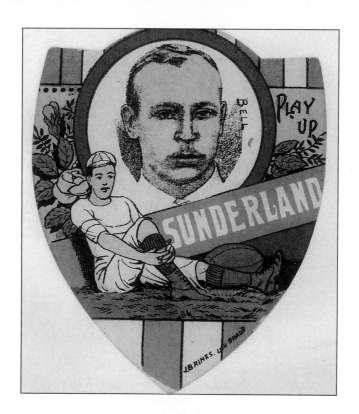

Roll of Honour

Football League Champions

1891-92
1892-93
1894-95
1901-02
1912-13
1935-36

FA Cup Winners

1937
1973

One
Early Days
1879-1900

Schooldays to Glory Days

Hendon Board School can stake a claim as the birthplace of football in Sunderland. When Scotsman James Allan took up a teaching post at the school he introduced the Association code to Wearside, where rugby had previously flourished. A meeting at the British Day School, Norfolk Street in October 1879 led to the formation of Sunderland and District Teachers' Association Football Club. For the first three seasons they played at the nearby Blue House Field before moving to Groves Field at Ashbrooke.

Former Hendon Board schoolboy Raich Carter after becoming the first Sunderland captain to receive the FA Cup. After being one of the top clubs in the country for half a century the Cup had always eluded Sunderland teams. After the Wembley triumph in 1937 Sunderland had to wait until 1973 before they won their next trophy. However, during this lean spell Sunderland were at times still the most famous club in England.

Sunderland line-up in 1884 kitted out in blue shirts and knickerbockers. Back row: Kirtley, McMillan, Lumsden, Singleton, Murdoch. Middle row: McDonald, J. Allan, Hall, Grayston, W.M. Allan. Front row: Leslie, Wade, Innes. During the 1883-84 season Sunderland played at the 'Clay Dolly Field' off Horatio Street at Roker. There were no dressing rooms so the players changed at The Wolseley public house nearby. At the end of the season Sunderland reached the Final of the Durham Challenge Cup. On 5 April 1884 they met Darlington at the old Cricket Ground, Newcastle Road. Before a crowd of between one and two thousand people Sunderland started playing 'up the hill'. At the end of an exciting contest Sunderland ran out 4-3 winners having trailed for most of the game. Darlington lodged a protest on the grounds their players had been intimidated by some of the home supporters. The referee also said he was threatened by three Sunderland players. This resulted in the Final being replayed at Birtley on 3 May. Cheap trips were organised by the North-Eastern Railway Company and many supporters took the opportunity to travel to see the match. Goals from Joyce and McDonald gave Sunderland a 2-0 victory to win the Cup 'again'. The following season the club moved to a new ground at Abbs Field in Fulwell. Sunderland reached the Durham Challenge Cup Final again and their opponents were again Darlington. The Quakers won the match 3-0 at Feethams and this time it was Sunderland's turn to protest at intimidation. The objections were dismissed and Darlington held on to the trophy.

Sunderland-born Charles W. Alcock was one of the most important figures in the history of football. He was appointed Secretary of the Football Association in 1870 at the age of 28. Within two years two momentous milestones had been achieved. In 1871 what was to become the most famous competition in the world was started – the FA Challenge Cup. The following year the first official international match took place – England played Scotland at Glasgow. A Sunderland man had laid the football foundations for the rest of the world to follow.

Before Sunderland entered the Football League they had already played in half a dozen FA Cup competitions. Sunderland's first tie was on 8 November 1884 at Redcar (the preliminary rounds were regional). Redcar won 3-1 and the following season Sunderland went out to the same club 3-0. Controversy was soon to dog Sunderland in the competition. They were disqualified in 1887-88 for playing three ineligible players against Middlesbrough. The following season they withdrew from the Cup rather than play Sunderland Albion. By the time Sunderland finally won the FA Cup they received a different trophy. The original cup was stolen when on display in a Birmingham shop window in 1895.

By 1885-86 Sunderland were playing in halved shirts which gave way to the famous red and white stripes by 1888. Back row: Wallace (secretary), Hunter, Turner (boot cleaner), Kirtley, Elliott, Todd (committee). Middle row: Marshall, Dale, Reed (chairman), McMillan. Front row: Erskine, Smith, Hornsby, Jobes, Smart. Sunderland were on the move again in April 1886 acquiring a field at Newcastle Road which they developed into a top class venue. This was an important period in Sunderland's history as men like shipbuilders Robert Thompson and James Marr and coal-owner Samuel Tyzack joined the club. The appointment of Tom Watson as secretary/manager was to signal the beginning of a golden age on Wearside built on the back of imported Scottish talent. At this time poaching players north of the border was a hazardous occupation with those caught receiving a severe beating. On one occasion Tyzack borrowed the clerical garb of Reverend McGonagle to avoid detection. The reward for this subterfuge was the assembling of one of the greatest sides in the land. Players brought south included: Johnny Campbell, Johnny Harvey and David Hannah from Renton; Tom Porteous and John Smith from Kilmarnock; Jack Scott from Coatbridge Albion Rovers and John Auld from Third Lanark. After a 7-2 victory over Aston Villa in a friendly in 1889, the Football League founder William McGregor was moved to say, 'Sunderland had a talented man in every position'. Thus even before Sunderland entered the League they had earned the title the 'Team of All the Talents'.

Sunderland Albion. Back row: Allison (committee), Campbell (trainer), McDermid, Angus, McFarlene, Coates (hon. secretary), Glass (vice-chairman). Middle row: Hannah, White, McNichol, Stewart, Brand. Front row: Smith, Weir, Kinnaird. Albion had been founded by James Allan and other disgruntled Sunderland members in March 1888. The new club attracted many of Sunderland's Scottish players which helped them to become quickly established on the field.

A card promoting the new club. In the 1888-89 season Sunderland were drawn against Sunderland Albion in both the FA Cup and Durham Cup. Rather than help swell their rivals' coffers Sunderland scratched from both competitions. The public on Wearside insisted on a showdown so the clubs agreed to meet in a friendly on 1 December 1888. A crowd of over 10,000 at Newcastle Road produced the first three figure gate receipts in the history of football in the region. The sum of £151 left each club with over £70 profit once expenses had been paid. Sunderland won the 'derby' clash 2-0.

Sunderland team of 1889-90, the last season before entering the League. Back row: Porteous, Kirtley, Watson (secretary), Oliver. Middle row: Harvey, Stevenson, Auld, Gibson, Scott. Front row: Smith, Campbell, Hannah. Eight of the players appeared in Sunderland's first ever League match on 13 September 1890. Scotsmen Harvey, Stevenson and Smith were replaced by fellow countrymen Wilson, Spence and Millar for the game.

A souvenir card dating from around 1890. Sunderland were one of the clubs featured in the series, with strip accuracy not always a major consideration. In the 1890-91 season Sunderland were admitted to the Football League at the expense of Stoke City. At this time footballers had to supplement their 25 shillings a week wages from football (10 shillings close season) with outside work. Sunderland players found work at the North Sands or Manor Quay shipyards, Dickinson's Engine Works and Wearmouth Foundry in Monk Street.

After playing in Sunderland's first ever League game Hugh Wilson went on to help the club to championship triumphs in 1891-92, 1892-93 and 1894-95. The long distances the Scottish international achieved with his one-handed throws caused havoc in opponents' goalmouths. This led to a change in the law and the introduction of the two-handed throw.

Like many of his fellow Scots Jimmy Millar was lured south by good wages, signing-on fees, match bonuses and some were even set up in business. After signing from Annbank in 1890 he was a regular in the Sunderland team that won three championships. In 1896 Millar joined Glasgow Rangers but returned to play an important part in the club's fourth title in 1901-02.

The famous Thomas Hemy painting of a Sunderland-Aston Villa game at Newcastle Road in 1895. The first match at the ground had been played on 3 April 1886 with Darlington providing the opposition. The club built up the stadium until it was the largest in the North East and in 1891 it staged the England-Wales match. After a dozen seasons at Newcastle Road the move was made to Roker Park.

Johnny Campbell was one of the greatest goalscorers of early League football. After signing from Scottish club Renton in 1889, the 5ft 7in, 13st, centre forward became the terror of English defences. He was the club's top scorer five times between 1890 and 1896. On three of these occasions he was also the top marksman in the entire League.

17

SUNDERLAND ASSOCIATION FOOTBALL CLUB COMMITTEE AND PLAYERS.

WINNERS OF LEAGUE CHAMP.ONSHIP.—SEASON 1894-95.

W. WALLACE,   T. DODDS,   R. McNEIL.   J. E. DOIG.   H.WILSON.   D. GOW.   A. McCREADIE.   Mr. JAS. HENDERSON.   H. REYNOLDS,
(Fin. Sec.)   (Trainer).   (Groundsman).
Mr. T. POTTS.   T. WATSON, (Sec.)   W. DUNLOP.   J. MILLER.   J. HANNAH.   J. HARVIE,   Coun. J. P. HENDERSON, (Presid.)   Coun. T. MARSHALL,
J. AULD.   J. GILLESPIE.   J. CAMPBELL.   J. SCOTT.   H. JOHNSTON.   Mr. S. WILSON.

Sunderland's third championship-winning side in four years. The team, with Scotsmen still to the forefront, also had a good Cup run. In the First Round Fairfield were swept away by a record 11-1 scoreline. Victories over Preston North End and Bolton Wanderers brought a semi-final meeting with Aston Villa. The Birmingham club were again to prove Sunderland's bogey team eventually going on to win the Cup.

Hailed as one of the finest left backs of his generation Jimmy Watson was to play over 200 League games for Sunderland between 1900 and 1907. He made four appearances for Scotland whilst at Roker and in one of these, against England, he played alongside team-mates Ted Doig and Andy McCombie. In April 1907 Watson moved to Middlesbrough, helping the Teessiders to the best defensive record in the League in his first season. His displays were also recognised at international level after an interval of four years. He was recalled for the match against Ireland in 1909 at the age of 31 and weighing 13½st. He was selected for the last time in the next game against England.

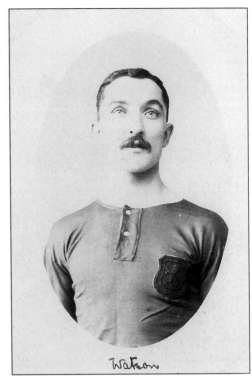

ANDREW McCOMBIE (SUNDERLAND).

Scotland international Andy McCombie was one of the best full backs in the game at the turn of the century. After six seasons with Sunderland he left in controversial circumstances. A dispute arose as to whether money given to McCombie by the club to start up a business was a gift or a loan. A court case and an FA inquiry followed and the club was fined and directors suspended. McCombie was transferred to neighbours Newcastle for a record £700 fee. At Gallowgate he added a further two caps to his collection before retiring in 1910. He then joined United's coaching staff where he remained for the next forty years.

19

After making his debut in Sunderland's third ever game in the League Ted Doig went on to become a legend on Wearside. Already a Scottish international with Arbroath he won a further three caps in a Roker career spanning fourteen seasons. His goalkeeping talents were still in demand in 1904 at the age of thirty-seven. Former Sunderland secretary Tom Watson took him to Liverpool. He made an immediate impact helping Liverpool to the Second Division title in his first season.

A postcard of a derby match at St James' Park. The scene depicted owes a fair amount to artistic licence. Sunderland's first League visit to Newcastle took place on 22 April 1899. A goal from McLatchie gave Sunderland a 1-0 victory.

Two

The New Century
1900-15

Another title
then almost the 'Double'

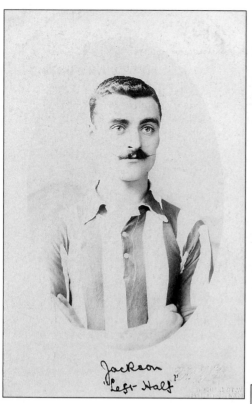

Jackson
"Left Half"

After winning an FA Amateur Cup medal with Middlesbrough Richard 'Dicky' Jackson joined Sunderland in the 1898 close season. Once he got established in professional football he went on to become Sunderland captain. His loyalty to the club was rewarded with a benefit on New Year's Eve 1904 which he shared with Billy Hogg.

The Sheffield Wednesday programme for Sunderland's League visit in the 1900-01 season. At the time Sunderland were top of the table with only two games left but a 1-0 defeat against Wednesday allowed Liverpool to snatch the title.

The team photograph from the programme celebrating the 1901-02 title. Although the cup in the picture is not the championship trophy. The team had got over the disappointment of being runners-up to Liverpool the previous season to bounce back as champions.

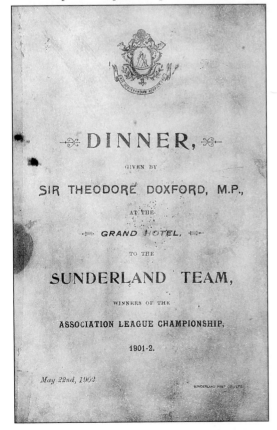

Sunderland MP Sir W. Theodore Doxford honoured a promise that if the club won the championship he would treat the players and officials to a celebration dinner. The Grand Hotel in Bridge Street hosted the event on 22 May 1902. In a speech, club chairman J.P. Henderson recalled how Sunderland had to travel something like 6,000 miles to achieve their triumph. On one occasion the team were stranded in York for several hours – 'that was fun in the depth of winter.'

Barrie
Centre Half

An unusual shot of Sunderland's squad in the 1902-03 season. It shows how Roker Park looked at the turn of the century. Although the capacity was a vast improvement on Newcastle Road, the low terracing and old grandstand could still not hold the massive crowds it was to later accommodate. The largest pre-First World War crowd was for West Bromwich Albion's FA Cup visit on 24 February 1912. The official attendance was 43,383 but many more climbed over the railings to get in. The second half had to be delayed because the crowd spilled onto the pitch.

After signing from Glasgow Park Head in the 1902 close season Alex Barrie found it difficult to break into the reigning champions side. He made only three appearances in the 1902-03 season but did score in the 4-2 win over Grimsby Town. After another four seasons in and out of the team he returned to Glasgow, this time to the mighty Rangers.

Jimmy Gemmell was joint leading scorer in the 1901-02 championship-winning side with 10 goals. Sunderland spotted his potential when he played against them in a friendly for Clyde. He was only 19 years old when he signed in November 1900 but he made rapid progress and was soon in the first team. In two spells with the club the skilful inside left made over 200 League appearances.

Sunderland-born Alf Common holds a unique place in English football, having been the first £500 transfer and the first four figure transfer. In 1900 he joined his hometown club but within eighteen months was on the move to Sheffield United for a fee of £325. Whilst with United the striker won two England caps and scored in an FA Cup Final. In 1904 he returned to Roker for £520. Eight months later Sunderland received £1,000 from Middlesbrough for Common's services.

A move from Willington Athletic to Sunderland in 1899 was to signal the start of a great career for Billy Hogg. A regular rather than prolific goalscorer, his talents were recognised at international level early on. He made his England debut against Wales in March 1902 when aged twenty-two.

Woolwich Arsenal v. Sunderland at Plumstead. 21.10.05.

A rare early action photograph of a League match between Woolwich Arsenal and Sunderland on 21 October 1905. The Londoners ran out 2-0 winners at the Manor Ground in Plumstead. Eight years after the game the Gunners made the controversial decision to move lock, stock and barrel across the river to their present home in North London.

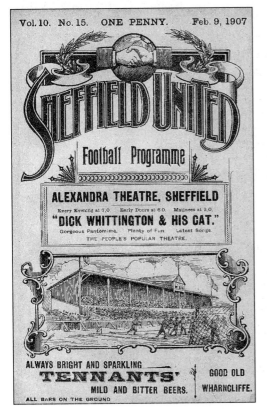

Vol. 10. No. 15.   ONE PENNY.   Feb. 9, 1907

SHEFFIELD UNITED

Football Programme

ALEXANDRA THEATRE, SHEFFIELD

Every Evening at 7.0.   Early Doors at 6.0.   Matinees at 2.0.

"DICK WHITTINGTON & HIS CAT."

Gorgeous Pantomime.   Plenty of Fun.   Latest Songs.
THE PEOPLE'S POPULAR THEATRE.

ALWAYS BRIGHT AND SPARKLING

TENNANTS'   GOOD OLD
MILD AND BITTER BEERS.   WHARNCLIFFE.
ALL BARS ON THE GROUND

Sheffield United's programme for the League game against Sunderland at Bramall Lane on 9 February 1907. Goals from McIntosh and Huggins could not prevent a 3-2 United victory. Having won at Roker earlier in the season the Blades thus completed the double over Sunderland.

Scenes from the FA Cup tie between Sunderland and Sheffield Wednesday on 23 February 1907. Before advances in printing technology allowed photographs of matches to appear in newspapers, sketches of the action were reproduced. A crowd of around 30,000 including over 700 from Wearside, witnessed a 0-0 draw. A few days later Wednesday snatched a 1-0 win in the replay at Roker. In 1914 Owlerton was renamed Hillsborough but the club are still known as the Owls.

Billy Agnew holds a special place in North East football as he was the first man to play for the 'Big Three' clubs. After joining Newcastle from Kilmarnock in 1902 he remained at St James' for two seasons before joining Middlesbrough. He then returned to Kilmarnock where he won three caps. In May 1908 he made his historic move to Roker Park.

Copyright Photograph by W. A. Culshaw, 119 High St. West, Sunderland.

SUNDERLAND ASSOCIATION FOOTBALL CLUB,
ROKER PARK.
League Champions : 1891-2, 1892-3, 1894-5, 1901-2.

A postcard for the 1908-09 season showing the players, the old stand at Roker Park and the Black Cat. Sunderland were to finish the campaign in third place in the League. The most notable performance by far was the record 9-1 win at Newcastle. The scoreline stunned the football world. The *Daily Express* reported, 'But for sheer amazement we have known nothing like the result at Newcastle for years... the result was due absolutely to the remarkable form of Sunderland. Surely this is the greatest performance ever known in football.'

WILLIAM HOGG,
SUNDERLAND A.F.C.

A solitary Billy Hogg goal was all that Sunderland had to show going into the half time interval against Newcastle United at St James' Park on 5 December 1908. When he and his team-mates walked off at full time he had completed his hat-trick and Sunderland had achieved an amazing victory.

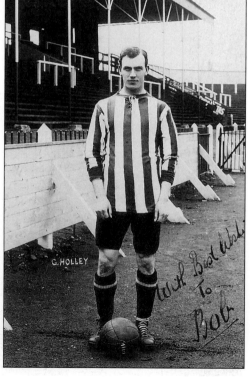

G. HOLLEY

George Holley was the first of Sunderland's two hat-trick men to complete the feat. The Seaham-born inside forward scored over 150 League and Cup goals for Sunderland. Four months after the Newcastle game he won the first of ten England caps (8 goals).

England winger Arthur Bridgett found the net twice in the 9-1 victory. For Bridgett some things came before football: he was involved with the Brotherhood Movement and was a much sought after preacher. He refused to play on Good Friday or Christmas Day because of religious convictions. Fortunately for Sunderland the 'St James' Massacre' fell on an 'ordinary' Saturday.

County Durham-born Jackie Mordue joined Sunderland from Arsenal in the 1908 close season. After barely a dozen League games he faced his first Tyne-Wear derby. He was to prove ready for the occasion: scoring Sunderland's eighth goal in the 73rd minute of the game. A few minutes later Hogg completed the scoring and Sunderland eased up for the last quarter of an hour of the game.

31

The only member of the forward line to fail to score in the Newcastle rout was England international Arthur Brown. Before joining the club from Sheffield United the centre forward had become one of the youngest players ever to represent his country. He was still only eighteen when he played against Wales in February 1904. His precocious talent had earned him the nickname 'Boy' Brown. It was not only his England credentials that brought Brown to Sunderland's attention. In October 1907 he scored four goals against Sunderland in a League game at Bramall Lane.

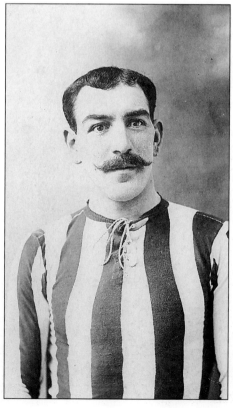

The imposing figure of Sunderland and Scotland captain Charlie Thomson. He was first capped with Hearts in 1904 and he continued as first choice centre half after his transfer to Sunderland in 1908. To secure his services Sunderland had to pay £700. At the time there was a transfer limit of £350 and the difference was made up by a make-weight player. His total of 21 caps was impressive in an age when internationals were limited to the Home Countries – three games a year.

Harry Martin made his debut for Sunderland on Good Friday 1912 and scored in the 2-1 defeat at Liverpool. Arthur Bridgett's refusal to play on religious grounds had left the door open for Martin's first appearance. The future England international never looked back while Bridgett never played for Sunderland again. The following month Bridgett was transferred to South Shields.

Carluke-born Tommy Tait might have thought international honours had passed him by during his fifth season at Roker. But at the age of thirty-one Scotland called him up for the international against Wales in March 1911. Although he never played for his country again the Sunderland wing half had achieved every footballer's dream.

In March 1911 Charlie Buchan was transferred from Southern League Leyton to Sunderland. On signing manager Bob Kyle told him: 'Son, it's very cold up north, so I advise you to get an outfit of thick winter clothes. You'll need them.' He took his advice and bought an outfit of warm clothes and was grateful he did: it was snowing when he arrived on Wearside and it did not stop for four days.

The Sunderland squad for the 1912-13 campaign. With the addition of a couple of signings in the October, these were the men who were to produce the most successful season ever in the club's history.

The Chelsea programme for Sunderland's visit to Stamford Bridge on 5 October 1912. This was the seventh League game of the season and Sunderland had still not recorded a win. The Pensioners ran out 2-0 victors providing another afternoon of disappointment for the Wearsiders. Charlie Buchan received a kick on the knee in the first five minutes and was a passenger on the wing before finally being forced to leave the field. Although the defeat sent Sunderland crashing to second off bottom in the table, from that point on they never looked back. As the season progressed Sunderland stormed up the League and clinched their fifth League title.

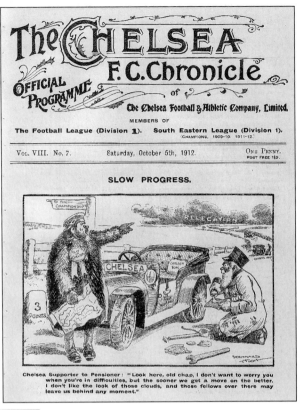

Making his debut in goal for Sunderland in the match at Stamford Bridge was Joe Butler. His transfer from Glossop was the turning point in Sunderland's fortunes. After the Chelsea defeat Sunderland won their next five games, scoring nineteen goals and conceding only three.

Charlie Gladwin made his debut in the match after the Stamford Bridge defeat. The physical presence of the barrel-chested full back settled the side and was a major factor in the championship success. The 6ft 1in, 14st former Blackpool man did have one unusual quirk: he overcame the problem of nerves by making himself sick before every game.

A post card of Sunderland's famous Black Cat mascot dating from before the First World War. When Sunderland played Newcastle in an FA Cup tie in March 1909 thousands of supporters made the short journey to St James' Park. The black cat with red and white ribbons attached was much in evidence among the 'invaders'. Sunderland's appearance in the 1913 FA Cup Final was another occasion which brought the lucky feline out in great numbers. The *Football Echo* reported how rail excursions from the area began shortly before midnight with supporters wearing their colours proudly. 'Sunderland's chief mascot was a miniature representation of the black cat, decked out with red and white ribbons, and many scores of these were carried by both sexes.'

A souvenir brochure of the 1913 FA Cup Final printed in Sunderland. It is now a collector's item and a copy recently changed hands for £700. This publication is sometimes mistaken for the Cup Final programme, which was a much less elaborate work.

After joining Sunderland from Barnsley in 1911 Harry Ness vied with Albert Milton for the left back spot. At times both played together with Ness switching to the other flank. An injury to Milton in the closing stages of the 1912-13 season allowed Ness to play in the semi-final replay and Final at Crystal Palace. By the time the war brought football to a halt he had made the position his own. He returned to play in Sunderland's first League match after the war.

The *London Illustrated News* featured the 1913 FA Cup Final. A huge crowd of 120,081 packed Crystal Palace to see the top two teams in England contest the Final. A late goal from Newcastle-born Tommy Barber gave Villa the Cup.

One of the major talking points of the Final was Charlie Thomson's clash with Villa centre forward Harry Hampton. Bad feeling between the pair had started in England-Scotland games and carried over into the Final. Although neither was sent off the FA suspended both men at the start of the following season. The First World War was to bring the curtain down on the Sunderland skipper's career. Even then the club wanted him to return for one more season after the war. After being demobbed he preferred to resume as landlord at the Black Bull Hotel at Prestonpans near Edinburgh.

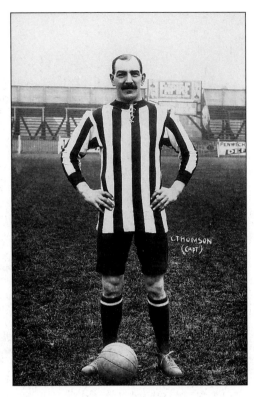

Four days after the Cup Final Walter Tinsley scored the goal in a 1-1 draw at Villa Park that virtually clinched the championship for Sunderland. For the top of the table clash he replaced George Holley who had played in the Final despite not being fully fit. After only a handful more appearances Tinsley was transferred to Exeter City at the end of the following season.

Action from a match in Budapest on Sunderland's tour in the summer of 1913. This was not the first time the Wearsiders had visited the city, four years before they played two games against local opposition, winning both matches. This time as reigning League champions there was extra responsibility on their shoulders to put up a good show.

Sunderland played three games in Budapest on the tour. They beat a Budapest XI (9-0) and a Hungary XI (3-2). The third encounter was against Blackburn Rovers who were also touring at that time. Even English opposition proved no obstacle for the Wearsiders. Sunderland finished their tour to the Austro-Hungarian Empire and Germany with a hundred per cent record from seven games.

Welsh international goalkeeper Leigh Richmond Roose joined Sunderland as an amateur in January 1908 having already appeared for Aberystwyth, London Welsh, Everton and Stoke City. He gave an impressive display against Woolwich Arsenal at Plumstead on 21 November 1908. The *Evening Standard* commented on his unique style. 'Roose, if he was tied down, could not explain any one of his methods: they are just methods of Roose. And they are his greatness. He is always Roose. And he is without a superior. No shot is impossible in his way of thinking, no danger too great to run.'

A promotional card given with the *Weekly Courier* bearing a caricature of Roose. Note the goalkeeper's jersey at the time was similar to outfield players. Roose's superb performances when taking over half way through the 1907-08 season were credited with keeping Sunderland up. At the start of the following season he was presented with a testimonial album on behalf of the inhabitants of Sunderland in appreciation of this. At the ceremony he recalled how many had asked what business he had to play for Sunderland, but it was not a business, it was a pleasure. He played for the love of the game and if he could not afford to play for pleasure he would not play at all. He had never played for pay and never would. In the derby match at St James' Park in November 1910 he broke his arm and never played for Sunderland again. He lost his life in the First World War.

41

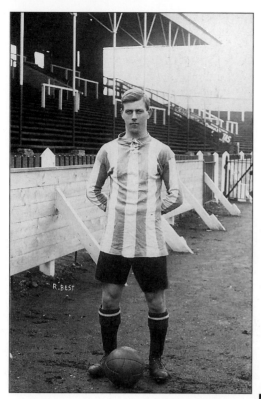

Bobby Best scored a hat-trick against Newcastle in the last League derby at St James' Park before the First World War. His goals helped Sunderland to a 5-2 victory on Christmas Day 1914. On a heavily sanded surface the Mickley-on-Tyne youngster scored his first goal after only eight minutes play. His second came on the half hour after holding off the challenge of three United men before slotting the ball home. Shortly after the interval he completed a memorable hat-trick.

Early in his goalkeeping career Walter Scott was known as the 'Penalty King' such was his reputation for saving spot-kicks. Sunderland signed the brilliant 'keeper from Everton for a fee of £750 in the summer of 1911. After being number one choice for most of his first season at the club things began to turn sour during his second campaign. Scott was blamed for a number of defeats and when he missed a training session after a mix up the club suspended him. He was then given a fortnight's notice on the grounds of 'palpable inefficiency'.

Sunderland's Cup run in 1913 brought Harry Low both joy and disappointment. He was chosen to play for Scotland against Ireland in Dublin on 15 March. However, Sunderland drew a replay with Newcastle and Low withdrew from the Scotland party to play in the second replay. He was never selected for his country again. In contrast brother Wilf won five caps whilst with Newcastle.

Presented with FOOTBALL SPECIAL, *September 30th, 1922.*

CHARLIE BUCHAN. Sunderland's six-foot star, hasn't had the caps he deserves, but is as popular as a Bank Holiday all over the country. Weighs 12 st. 6 lbs.

OUR FOOTBALL BOYS—No. 4.

The gangling figure of Charlie Buchan gave cartoonists plenty of material to work with. At the start of his first full season at Sunderland he stood 5ft 9½in and weighed 10st 5lb. Three months later his weight had remained the same but he had shot up to 6ft¾in. This rapid gain in height left him weak during matches and it also sapped his confidence. He walked out on Sunderland and returned to Woolwich. Bob Kyle persuaded him to return and once he put on a couple of stones in weight he was back to his best.

Having finally established himself as first choice left back after his transfer from Barnsley in 1908, Albert Milton looked forward to the 1912-13 season with high hopes. With little over a month of the campaign remaining he had been an ever present in the side, but an injury in the match against Manchester City in 22 March 1913 robbed him of an FA Cup Final place and was to effectively signal the end of his Roker career. He received a benefit from the club the following season and then moved on to Swindon. Like former team-mate Roose, the Rotherham-born full back was killed in the war.

Before the First World War Billy Cringan was just beginning to establish himself in the Sunderland side. In 1915 the club sold him to Celtic to help them through a bad financial patch. With the suspension of the League programme at the end of the 1914-15 season Sunderland could no longer rely on a regular income from gate receipts. After the war Cringan went on to become a Scottish international.

Three

Between the Wars
1919-39

The Cup at last

Joe Kasher signed for Sunderland in May 1919 and was the club's regular centre half in the early post-war seasons. The County Durham man had been a Prisoner of War in Germany for the latter part of hostilities. After returning home Kasher played for Crook Town but appeared as a guest player for Sunderland in the Victory League in 1919. He then played against Sunderland for Crook in the Final of the Durham Senior Cup. Despite being on the wrong end of an 8-0 scoreline Kasher impressed the Sunderland officials and he was signed on.

F. CUGGY

Frank Cuggy along with Charles Buchan and Jackie Mordue made up the famous 'Sunderland Triangle'. They formed a brilliant understanding on the pitch which led to the trio performing together at international level in Belfast in 1913. Unfortunately the result did not go their way and Ireland recorded their first ever victory over England. However, Cuggy was selected for the corresponding fixture the following year.

The Sunderland squad for the 1919-20 season, the first after the First World War. The Armistice had come too late for the 1918-19 season to get underway but there was a Victory League at the turn of the year. Along with Sunderland seven other local clubs took part. The club made a profit of £2,556 on these games which helped to pay for restoring Roker Park after the neglect of the war years.

Barney Travers scorer of two goals in the first League derby at St James' after the First World War. With a quarter of an hour of the match remaining United led 2-1 when Travers levelled the score. The *Newcastle Daily Journal* reported, 'with five minutes to go Travers got clear away with a great solo effort, and though tackled by McCracken, he scored with a magnificent drive, winning the game for the Wearsiders.' His goals before a crowd of 61,761 earned Sunderland a 3-2 win and completed a double over their old rivals. The previous week the Magpies were beaten by two Charlie Buchan goals at Roker.

The Aston Villa programme for the League encounter with Sunderland on 12 February 1921. Sunderland recorded a 5-1 win over their old rivals with goals from Buchan (2), Marshall (2) and an own goal. Buchan's first goal came after a piece of 'masterful dribbling'. The Sunderland centre forward almost completed a hat-trick as he also struck an upright.

Despite losing four years to the war Charlie Buchan made over four hundred League and Cup appearances for Sunderland. His goalscoring record at Roker was also impressive with better than a goal every two games. In the summer of 1925 Buchan was involved in an extraordinary move to Arsenal. Rather than a set fee Sunderland would receive £2,000 plus £100 for every goal Buchan scored in his first season at Highbury. Fortunately Buchan scored 21 goals and Sunderland, who had wanted £4,000 for the thirty-three-year-old player, received a bonus.

Scottish international centre half Michael Gilhooley was transferred from Hull City on 2 March 1922 for a fee of £5,250. He had an injury-plagued Roker career and only made twenty League appearances in over two years.

On the same day as Gilhooley signed for Sunderland Jock Paterson joined the club from Leicester City. A free-scoring centre forward Paterson was also a Scottish international at the time. Sunderland's mid-table position prompted manager Bob Kyle to delve into the transfer market.

W. CRESSWELL.

The football world had barely had time to overcome the shock of the double transfer swoop when the following day Sunderland signed Warney Cresswell. South Shields were paid £5,500 for the England full back. All three newcomers made their debut in the game against Sheffield United at Roker on 4 March. The new blood helped Sunderland to a 1-0 victory with the goal coming from 'old boy' Charlie Buchan.

A. DONALDSON
SUNDERLAND

The big money spending had still not been completed: at the end of March Alex Donaldson was bought from Bolton Wanderers. The Scottish international winger was to play only one full season at Sunderland before moving on to Manchester City. Sunderland had spent over £20,000 in a month but of the international quartet only Cresswell was to prove a long-term success at Roker.

Copyright Arthur Hackett.   SUNDERLAND A.F.C., 1922-23.   49 Grey St., Newcastle on Tyne.
FERGUSON.   CRESSWELL.   ENGLAND.   ROBSON.   HAWES.   POOLE.
R. H. KYLE (Sec.).   DONALDSON.   BUCHAN.   PARKER (Capt.).   PATERSON.   ELLIS.   W. WILLIAMS (Trainer)

The Sunderland squad in the 1922-23 season which finished runners-up to Liverpool for the championship. The strike force of Buchan and Paterson was to prove a lethal combination. Buchan's 30 League goals made him the country's leading marksman. Paterson contributed another 21 goals to Sunderland's total of 72.

Centre forward Paterson looks on as the Blackburn 'keeper Davis claims the ball in the match at Ewood Park on 23 September 1922. In his first full season after leaving Leicester Paterson finished with a total of 24 League and Cup goals. This was to be the high point of his Roker career, in October 1924 he was transferred to Preston North End.

Charlie Parker closes in on a Blackburn Rovers player in the same match at Ewood Park in 1922. Record signing from South Shields, Warney Cresswell looks on. Two other expensive acquisitions – Jock Paterson and Alex Donaldson were also in the side that drew 0-0 with Rovers.

Left: Ernie England is beaten to the ball by a Chelsea player. The Sunderland full back was an ever present during the 1922-23 season. Calls for him to be recognised at international level went unheeded. Right: Soaring above the Chelsea defence Charlie Buchan heads for goal.

Sunderland's Billy Moore can claim to have played before the biggest crowd in history. In 1912 he joined the club from Seaton Delaval on amateur forms. He made his League debut against Sheffield United on 7 February 1914. In that year he travelled with the England Amateur team on two Continental tours. He scored two goals on his debut in a 8-1 win over Belgium in Brussels and in two games against Sweden in Stockholm he found the net three times. After appearing in a defeat in Denmark he ended his amateur career and signed professional with Sunderland in August 1914. He was beginning to make his way in the first team when the war halted matters. After the resumption he returned to Roker Park but could never establish a regular place in the side. In May 1922 Sunderland transferred him to West Ham United and within a year he was turning out in the first Wembley Cup Final against Bolton Wanderers.

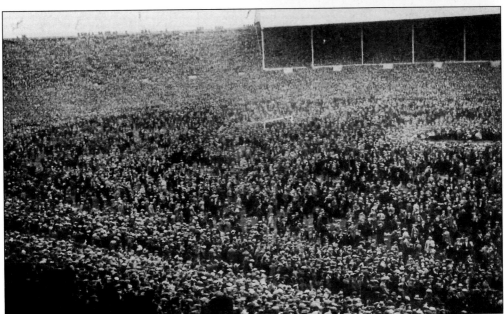

The official attendance for the 1923 Cup Final was 127,000 but some estimates put the figure as high as a quarter of a million. People continued to surge through the gates long after the capacity had been reached. The huge crowd was forced on to the pitch and the start was delayed. Despite finishing up on the losing side at Wembley Billy Moore's new career continued to flourish when he played for England. After his playing days were over he became West Ham's trainer and stayed at the club up to 1960.

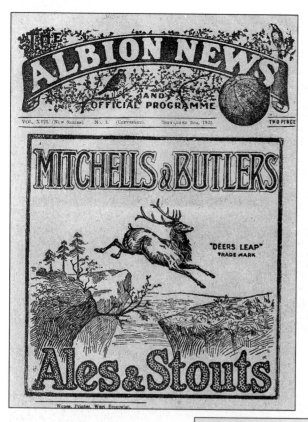

The West Bromwich Albion programme for Sunderland's League visit on 5 September 1925. Sunderland had made an impressive start to the season with home wins over Birmingham (3-1) and Blackburn Rovers (6-2). This continued at the Hawthorns with Dave Halliday notching a hat-trick and Coglin and Ellis also each finding the net in a 5-2 victory. The next game brought a 6-1 win against Sheffield United at Roker but then more erratic form set in. Sunderland eventually finished the season in third place in the League.

Sunderland's good form owed much to Dave Halliday who scored ten goals in the first four games of the season. He finished the 1925-26 season with 38 League goals with a further four in the FA Cup. The Scottish centre forward still holds the Sunderland record for the most League goals in one season. His 43 goals in the 1928-29 campaign also made him the country's leading goalscorer.

Bell in the Sunderland goal comes under pressure from Manchester United's attack during a League match at Roker Park on 30 November 1929. At this time Sunderland were in a period of transition, with manager Johnny Cochrane having taken over only the previous season.

The Sunderland 'keeper had a busy afternoon despite the home side taking an early lead through Gunson. After Joe Spence equalised Manchester United took control with Spence scoring a second and Hanson and Ball stretching the lead. Morrison pulled a late goal back to make the final score 4-2 to United.

An unusual picture of Sunderland's line-up before the start of the 1930-31 season. Left to right: Billy Eden, Billy Clunas, Tommy Urwin, Bill Murray, Bobby Gurney, Jock McDougall, Paddy Bell, Patsy Gallacher, Harold Shaw, Arthur Andrews, Jimmy Connor. The only change in the team that opened the campaign with a 3-3 draw at home to Manchester City was Bob Robinson replaced Bell in goal.

The Portsmouth programme for the League match with Sunderland on 6 September 1930. The third game of the season was to produce Sunderland's third draw. If a return of only a point a game was a disappointment worse was to follow – five successive defeats. Despite these set-backs Sunderland ended the season in a respectable mid-table position.

Sunderland's Scottish international goalkeeper Bob Middleton in action at Stamford Bridge in 1930. The legendary Hughie Gallacher was the star of the show when Sunderland visited the capital for a League game on 13 December. Having signed from Newcastle only a few months before Scotland's diminutive centre forward scored two of Chelsea's goals in a 5-0 drubbing.

When Bill Murray joined Sunderland in April 1927 from Cowdenbeath he had no idea that he would spend all but two of the next thirty years at Roker Park. After nine years as the club's right back he moved back to Scotland with St Mirren. In 1938 he returned to take over from Johnny Cochrane as manager. He resigned in 1957 having just failed on a number of occasions to bring silverware to the club.

Before joining Sunderland from Aberdeen Benny Yorston had been compared with the great Hughie Gallacher. He had topped the Scottish League goalscoring charts in the 1929-30 season with 38 goals in 38 games. Sunderland paid £2,000 to lure the 5ft 5in Scottish international to Roker in January 1932. Despite scoring seven goals in his first five games for Sunderland Yorston's stay was to be brief. Fierce competition for places in the forward line from men like Gurney, Gallacher and Carter made him surplus to requirements and he was allowed to move on to Middlesbrough.

In February 1930 Sunderland were chasing the signature of Harold Shaw of Wolves when Newcastle made an inquiry. Wolves upped the price and Sunderland had to pay a record fee for a left back – £7,000. Ironically Shaw made his debut in the derby at St James' Park on 22 February. Despite a brilliant individual performance from the new signing Sunderland went down to a 3-0 defeat.

The West Bromwich goalkeeper drops on the ball as Bobby Gurney is about to shoot for goal. The League game at Roker Park on 11 September 1935 ended in a 6-1 Sunderland victory. The star of a brilliant performance was Raich Carter who notched four goals.

After signing from Bradford Park Avenue in April 1932 Bert Davis only missed five League games in the next three seasons. He was in and out of the 1935-36 championship-winning side but still scored 10 goals. The low point of that season came in the match against Middlesbrough at Ayresome Park. Raich Carter was sent off for the only time in his career and when Davis said something to the referee he followed him for an early bath.

The Birmingham City programme for Sunderland's visit on 13 April 1936. A brilliant 7-2 victory ensured Sunderland claimed the First Division title. The score could have been much higher as the home 'keeper made a dozen outstanding saves. The *Newcastle Journal* correspondent reported, 'I have had nearly 40 years of first class football, but I have never seen a team toyed with to the extent Birmingham were in this match.'

Bobby Gurney scorer of four goals at St Andrews which helped Sunderland equal Aston Villa's record of six titles received a special welcome on his return to Wearside. A crowd of 50,000 awaited the players arrival home. When the team emerged from the Central Railway Station there were shouts of 'Next Year Bobby' referring to the FA Cup being the next target. After joining Sunderland from Bishop Auckland in 1925 Bobby went on to become one of the club's all-time greats. His whole-hearted centre forward play was rewarded with over two hundred League and Cup goals. His displays were also recognised at international level winning an England cap against Scotland.

Jarrow-born Jimmy Thorpe tragically died four days after being injured in a League game against Chelsea in 1936. The young goalkeeper received kicks to the head and body in a goalmouth scramble at Roker Park on Saturday, 1 February. Although dazed he finished the match but took ill on the Monday. He was taken to hospital but lapsed into a coma and died on the Wednesday. The twenty-two-year-old suffered from diabetes but the coroner said the rough treatment contributed to his death.

Sunderland with the 1935-36 championship trophy. Back row: Carter, Thomson, Hall, Mapson, Hastings, Collin, Clarke. Front row: Cochrane (manager), Davis, Gurney, Gallacher, Connor, Reid (trainer).

CHAIRMAN: ALD. SIR WALTER RAINE, KT., J.P.

The Town Council honoured the 1935-36 championship-winning team with a celebration dinner at the New Rink. Vice-chairman Duncan White presented the players with their winners' medals before 350 guests. There was an emotional moment when he called up Jimmy Thorpe's father to receive his son's medal.

An aerial view of Roker Park in 1936. At the time the old Clockstand (left) was being rebuilt. Archibald Leitch was the architect, the same man who had designed the Main Stand (right) a few years before. Almost thirty years later a roof was put over the Fulwell End (top). The concrete supports of the Roker End (bottom) became structurally unsafe in 1982 and had to be partially demolished.

The Sunderland team dressed in the height of 1930s fashion pose under the Roker End. Between 1912 and 1913 the Roker End had been erected at a cost of £20,000. The massive concrete supports were an innovation as up to then terracing was cut from earth banking or built on wood or steel supports. In 1902 twenty-six people had died when wooden terracing collapsed at Ibrox Park during an England-Scotland game.

Scottish international inside forward Patsy Gallacher was a great favourite of the Roker crowd. His goal in the semi-final against Millwall put Sunderland into the Final. In November 1938 the twenty-eight-year-old was transferred to Stoke for £5,500. He had just received his second benefit cheque for £650 from Sunderland, having completed ten years with the club. He thought a change of surroundings would do him good.

Sandy McNab was the only change from the semi-final side to that which turned out at Wembley. Alex Hastings was the unlucky man to lose out, he had been injured in a game just before the Cup run began. Fellow Scot McNab then played in all seven Cup games up to the semi.

A Sunderland supporter takes a break in the streets of London on Cup Final Day 1937. Sunderland's allocation was limited to just 10,000 tickets. Roker Park was inundated with postal applications at least four times that number. Some supporters had followed the team in every round. Long journeys to Southampton, Luton, Wolverhampton, Sheffield and Huddersfield, counted for nothing. Even a number of season ticket holders were too late with their applications and missed out. For weeks the local press was full of correspondence on the subject. Rumours of Cup tickets abounded on Wearside in the run up to the Final. Roker and Fulwell British Legion had a letter published in the *Echo* denying they had received a batch of 200 tickets from Sunderland AFC. They declared they had received absolutely none.

An unusual shot of Sunderland's team prior to going to Wembley. Who are the Sunderland players doing the Ravanelli impersonations almost sixty years before the Italian striker arrived on Teesside? Answers on the next page.

Back row: Hall, Thomson (partly hidden), Hastings, Carter, Gurney. Middle: Johnston, Burbanks, McNab. Front: Gorman, Mapson, Duns.

Just before the kick-off 2s 6d (12½p) tickets were changing hands for 15s (75p). All but 1,800 of Sunderland's 10,000 allocation were for tickets under 5s (25p). At the upper end of the market guinea (£1.05) tickets were fetching £5 5s (£5.25). Preston North End had the same allocation of tickets as Sunderland yet the crowd numbered 93,495.

The 1937 FA Cup Final programme. Sunderland's path to the Final was not without its jitters. The quarter-final clash with Wolves was an epic struggle. A 1-1 draw at Molineux was followed by a 2-2 stalemate at Roker. In the decider at Hillsborough goals from Carter, Gurney, Gallacher and Thomson finally eased Sunderland into the semi.

The Sunderland goal under intense pressure from the Preston attack in the 1937 Final. On this occasion they managed to get the ball clear. The defence was breached before the interval when Scottish international Frank O'Donnell put Preston ahead.

A panoramic view of the Final. A second half fight back saw Sunderland score three times without reply. A Gurney header pulled the sides level and then goals from Carter and Burbanks sealed Sunderland's triumph. Note the old roof only covered the seated area of the ground. Improvements completed for the 1966 World Cup included a new roof which sheltered all spectators from the elements.

Sunderland's Black Cat was depicted in a series of cigarette cards in 1933. The reverse of the card noted that even at that time Sunderland were less gloriously known as the 'Wearsiders' or the 'Rokerites'. Twelve-year-old Sunderland supporter Billy Morris smuggled a black kitten into the 1937 Final to help bring his favourites luck. The red and white adorned cat stayed in the youngster's coat pocket during the game.

The Roker Roar on tour 1937 style. A supporter down for the Final shows that fancy dress at Sunderland matches is not a modern day phenomenon.

A crucial factor in Sunderland's Cup win was the performance of Bert Johnston against the Preston number nine. Although Frank O'Donnell scored in the first half the Sunderland centre half had his measure for most of the game. When his playing days were over Johnston remained at Roker Park by joining the training staff.

The Queen congratulates Raich Carter before presenting him with the trophy that had for so long been a stumbling block for Sunderland. The Sunderland skipper, who a few day before had been married, received a special message when handed the Cup. The Queen said, 'That is a nice wedding present for you.'

SUNDERLAND CUP TEAM 1936-37.
THOMSON. GORMAN. JOHNSTON. MAPSON. HALL. HASTINGS.
JOHN COCHRANE. CARTER. GURNEY. GALLACHER. A. REID.
(SEC. MANAGER.) (TRAINER.)
DUNS. ARTHUR HACKETT BURBANKS.
Copyright.

The Sunderland eleven that beat Millwall 2-1 in the 1937 FA Cup semi-final at Huddersfield, Sandy McNab replaced Alex Hastings for the Final.

The celebrations begin: Left to right: Billy Dunlop (assistant trainer), Jimmy Gorman, Andy Reid (trainer), Len Duns, Raich Carter with the Cup, Sandy McNab and Bert Johnston.

A composite photograph of the team with the FA Cup. Sunderland included five Scotsmen in the Wembley side. Another Scot in the Preston side was to become even more famous as a manager – Bill Shankley.

Sunday Graphic and Sunday News, May 2, 1937.

TRUTH ABOUT BUDGET PANIC: By BEVERLEY BAXTER, M.P.

SUNDAY GRAPHIC
and SUNDAY NEWS

BEAUTY FOR ALL: GREAT NEW SERIES

RADIO P. 28

No. 1,152.   [Registered as a newspaper.]   SUNDAY, MAY 2, 1937.   TWOPENCE.

HIS FINAL WEDDING GIFT
The Queen Presents The Cup to Sunderland's Captain

Sunderland's cup victory made front page news the day after the Final. Despite having won six League titles, losing finalists in 1913 had been the closest Sunderland had been to winning the FA Cup.

The Sunderland and Celtic teams for the friendly at Roker Park on 6 October 1937. The Scottish Cup-holders beat their English counterparts by a score of 2-0. One of the goalscorers was Jimmy McGrory who was to retire the following year after scoring a record 550 goals in first-class football. McGrory's goalscoring record for Celtic was phenomenal: in 378 League games he scored 397 goals. In contrast to Sunderland's solitary Cup win at that time Celtic had won their competition on no less than fifteen occasions. The Sunderland and Celtic teams together with the English and Scottish Cups. Back row: Gorman, Delaney, McDowall, Crum, Burbanks, Murphy. Third row: Reid (trainer), Hall, Hogg, Mapson, Peterson, Doyle, McDonald, Johnston, McMenemy (trainer). Second row: Johnny Cochrane (manager), Gurney, McGrory, Carter, Lyon, Gallacher, Maley (manager). Front row: Duns, Buchan, Thomson, Morrison. The Celtic players had watched Sunderland's victory at Wembley in recognition of their Cup triumph the previous week. Despite Sunderland having a large Scottish contingent in their ranks the Celtic players were supporting their opponents in the Final. Former Celtic men Frank and Hugh O'Donnell were in the Preston side that day.

Arsenal goalkeeper Boulton beats Bobby Gurney to the ball in the League match at Highbury on 18 September 1937 before a 60,000 crowd. In the corresponding fixture three seasons before, Sunderland's visit had set Arsenal's record attendance. With the Gunners chasing their third successive League title, 73,295 had packed Highbury for the match.

Boulton again foils the Sunderland attack, this time Raich Carter comes off second best. The match produced an amazing goalscoring burst. Milne put Arsenal ahead after three minutes play and within five minutes were 4-0 up. England centre forward Ted Drake, Hulme and Davidson all found the net. Only a further two minutes had passed when Bobby Gurney pulled a goal back. The star-studded Arsenal and Sunderland sides could not add to the scoreline in the remaining 75 minutes.

Sunderland 'keeper Matt Middleton saves a shot from Milne. The Gunners' line-up for the match included eight England internationals: Drake, Bastin, Hulme, Copping, Roberts, Crayston, Hapgood and Male.

The Tottenham programme on the occasion of the record-breaking gate at White Hart Lane on 5 March 1938. Cup holders Sunderland stood between Spurs and a semi-final spot. On a warm sunny afternoon 75,038 crammed into the stadium with over 10,000 locked out.

The Spurs defence comes under pressure from one of the most feared attacks in the country during the Cup tie. It was the Londoners third successive appearance in the quarter-finals.

Spurs' goalkeeper Hooper and defender Hall repel a Sunderland attack in the record-breaking Cup tie at White Hart Lane.

Gibbons of Spurs gets in a shot on the Sunderland goal but Mapson clears. Sunderland had gone twelve games undefeated in the competition before the Tottenham game and the thirteenth was not to prove unlucky. A great goal from Raich Carter ten minutes from time settled the issue.

Four

Wartime
1939-45

Phoney war to real bombs
on Roker Park

Eddie Burbanks scored in Sunderland's last League game before the war. The match at Highbury on 2 September 1939 was put back to a 5 p.m. kick-off because of traffic congestion. The day before the task of evacuating three million mothers, children and the disabled from the large cities had got underway. The game itself was a rout with Ted Drake scoring four goals in a 5-1 Arsenal win. The following day Britain declared war on Germany and the League programme ended for the duration.

Birkenhead-born Johnny Mapson was signed from Reading a month after Jimmy Thorpe's tragic death. He made the keeper's jersey his own until the war brought a halt to proceedings. The former Reading 'keeper toured South Africa in the summer of 1939 with an England party. He played in two Test matches against the Springboks, winning 8-2 in Durban and 2-1 in Johannesburg. Mapson appeared for England in a wartime international against Wales on 26 April 1941. The game at Nottingham ended in a 4-1 victory to England.

Before the war Raich Carter won every honour in the game with Sunderland. After serving in the Auxiliary Fire Service for two years at the start of the war Carter moved on to the RAF. In December 1945 he joined Derby County with whom he found immediate success. In his first season he helped the Rams to an FA Cup Final victory at Wembley. In March 1948 he set out on a new challenge as player-assistant manager at Hull City.

PASTIMES OF OUR KING
AT INTERNATIONAL FOOTBALL MATCH.

The Duke of York (later George VI) meets Raich Carter and the rest of the England players before an international. The England captain doing the introductions was Tommy 'Snowy' Cooper who was to die in a motor cycle crash while serving with the Military Police in 1940. Despite winning thirteen full caps Carter's international career was decimated by the war. He won the last of his six caps whilst with Sunderland on 17 April 1937. It was to be almost ten years before he made his next appearance now playing for Derby. He wasted no time in resurrecting his England career playing in the first seven full internationals after the war.

Action from the first leg of the War League Cup Final against Wolves at Roker Park on 23 May 1942. This competition had replaced the FA Cup which had been suspended for the duration. A crowd of 32,113 saw Sunderland held to a 2-2 draw by the Midlanders. One of Sunderland's scorers was Newcastle United's Albert Stubbins who was playing as a guest. Stubbins was the leading marksmen in wartime football in England with well over two hundred goals. Stubbins' haul included a remarkable run of four hat-tricks in succession.

Wolves 'keeper Sidlow manages to keep the ball out during the first leg game at Roker. Raich Carter found the net in the first match and the England international also scored in the second leg at Molineux before 43,038 people. However, this was not enough as Wolves ran out 4-1 winners to lift the trophy.

A photograph from the Luftwaffe archives shows how perilous Roker Park's location was in terms of 'targets' such as Sunderland's shipyards and docks.

An air raid on 16 May 1943 caused damage to the pitch and also to the Main Stand. The old club house on the corner of Roker Baths Road was destroyed. A special constable was killed in a street near the ground. After a raid a couple of months before when a bomb also landed on the pitch the German High Command announced, 'on the night of March 14, a formation of fast bomber aircraft made a strong attack against the shipbuilding centre of Sunderland.'

Colonel Joe Prior served as Sunderland chairman during the war years. The Colonel had fought in both the Boer War and the First World War. When he travelled to Scotland with manager Bob Kyle intending to buy a player, he bought a horse. First appointed to the board in 1919 he served the club for thirty years. A well-known figure on Wearside his name lives on in the Colonel Prior public house at Doxford Park.

Left to right: Arthur Wright, Len Duns and Arthur Housam. The locally-born trio all had their Roker careers interrupted by the war. They all played wartime football with Sunderland and then resumed playing League football after hostilities. Between September 1939 and the end of the war forty Sunderland players had joined the forces. Many former players also served, like Johnny Lynas who made a number of appearances for Sunderland in 1928-29 season. He was taken prisoner by the Japanese at the fall of Singapore and worked in a Prisoner of War hospital in Thailand for the rest of the war.

Five

Bank of England Club
1946-58

Money can't buy success

Eddie Burbanks in action against Manchester United. Old Trafford was severely damaged during air raids and United shared Maine Road with rivals City for a period after the war. It was while at their temporary home that United set the all-time attendance record for a League game – 83,260 for the visit of Arsenal in January 1948. Having scored in the last game before the war Burbanks also found the mark in Sunderland's first League game after the resumption. He scored in Sunderland's 3-2 victory over Derby County seven years after the Arsenal game.

Sunderland's team for the League visit to Bramall Lane on 11 October 1947. Back row: Scotson, Wright, Stelling, Mapson, Hudgell, Walsh. Front row: Duns, Robinson, Davis, Watson, Reynolds. In the early part of the game a number of Sunderland passes went to the red and white stripes of United instead of to unfamiliar white-shirted team-mates. Despite this Sunderland led 2-0 at half-time through goals from Davis and Reynolds. The home side stormed back to earn a 3-2 victory, with the United 'keeper saving a Reynolds penalty.

Opposite: Old and New Boys: Left to right: Len Duns, Tommy McLain, W. Cook (trainer), Fred Hall, Len Shackleton. Duns had been with Sunderland since 1933 while the other three players were all post-war signings.

Johnny Mapson in action during a Sunderland-Chelsea game at Stamford Bridge in 1947. In November 1945 82,000 people crammed into the ground for the visit of Moscow Dynamo. With the gates locked many spectators took up precarious positions on the roof. In 1955 it was Roker Park's turn to entertain the famous Russian club.

Sunderland's Ronnie Turnbull made one of the most sensational debuts in Football League history. When he was chosen for the game against Portsmouth at Roker Park on 29 November 1947 he could not have dared dream of the eventual outcome. After twenty minutes he scored his first goal, followed by another ten minutes later. Early in the second half he completed his hat-trick. Pompey pulled a goal back but the debut-boy had the last word when he scored his fourth shortly before the final whistle. Despite finding the net again in his next match the goal flood was then reduced to a trickle. In September 1949 he was transferred to Manchester City.

Supporters stream across the Wearmouth Bridge after the match against Arsenal on 18 September 1948. A crowd of 64,436 had set new League attendance figures for Roker Park. The record was not to last long, Blackpool's visit the following season surpassed the Gunners' total.

Sunderland squad at the start of the 1949-50 season. Back row: Scarth, R. Robinson, McClurkie, Mapson, McLain. Second row: Jones (third team trainer), Gray (senior trainer), Oliver, Davis, Marston, Ramsden, Hall, Scotson, A. Wright, Hudgell, Johnston (reserve trainer). Third row: J. Robinson, Turnbull, Broadis, Duns, Bill Murray (manager), Stelling, L. Shackleton, Dunn, Walsh. Front row: J. Shackleton, Dougall, T. Wright.

Derby County 'keeper Townsend takes the ball off Tommy Wright in the match at Roker Park on 21 January 1950. A crowd of 62,413 gathered to see if Sunderland could maintain their title challenge. During the season over one million people attended matches at Roker Park.

Johnny Mapson holds off a challenge from Derby's Morris. Sunderland ran out easy 6-1 winners with Dickie Davis notching a hat-trick. Going into the final month of the season Sunderland were favourites to lift the title. But a home defeat against lowly Manchester City was to cost Sunderland the championship.

Sunderland players and officials boarding a chartered plane at London Airport bound for Istanbul in May 1950. A party from Hull City shared the flight, with the players from both clubs having to be insured for £1,000,000 for the journey.

On the journey to Turkey the Sunderland party had an overnight stop-over in Rome. Len Shackleton recalled how the peace of the night was broken with the sound of breaking glass. His fear of an anti-British attack on the hotel were eased when he discovered team-mate Reg Scotson was the cause of the commotion. He had opened one of the windows and not realising it was double glazed put his head through the second pane. Reg survived the incident without any serious injury.

Johnny Mapson goes in bravely against the Galatasaray captain in the third game of the Turkish tour. In the first match Len Shackleton scored a hat-trick against Besiktas before a sell-out crowd of 25,000.

Shackleton, ball and goalkeeper all end up in the Galatasaray net on the way to a 4-3 victory. Sunderland not only finished the tour with a hundred per cent record but their style of football won many friends. After the last match the Turks said they had been given lessons in the game by 'masters of football'.

On returning from Turkey Willie Watson discovered he had been selected for England's World Cup party for Brazil. A stylish footballer who could play in a variety of positions, Willie was one of the game's gentlemen. As well as representing his country at football he also played Test cricket.

Sunderland team in the 1950-51 season. Back row: Gray (trainer), A. Wright, Hall, McLain, Mapson, Ford, Shackleton, Walsh. Front row: T. Wright, Davis, Hedley, Hudgell.

The Sunderland and Galatasaray teams line up before a friendly at Roker Park on 11 September 1950. Four months before the Istanbul club had played hosts to Sunderland. A crowd of 14,830 turned out with the hope of seeing some 'Eastern promise'.

Sunderland skipper Len Duns receives a pennant from his opposite number of Galatasaray before the kick-off. Sunderland again proved too strong for the Turkish side, goals from Kirtley, Duns and Davis completed a comfortable 3-1 victory.

The eighteen-year-old Galatasaray 'keeper Turgay Seren in action at Roker. The youngster went on to become a big star in Turkish football, playing for his country on more than fifty occasions.

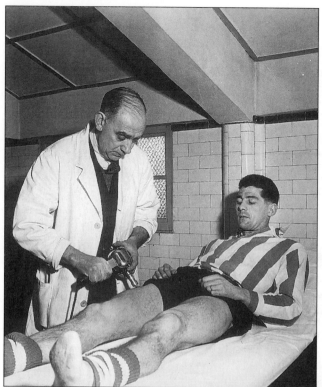

Trevor Ford on the treatment table. Alex Wilson, the former Arsenal goalkeeper, was Sunderland's first qualified physiotherapist. Up to that time the job of treating injuries fell to the trainer. As early as 1930 there was a special treatment room at Roker Park with 'sun-ray' equipment to 'tone up the system'.

Trevor Ford is presented with a Welsh cap in the Roker dressing-room as team-mates Len Shackleton and Willie Watson look on. On 15 November 1950 Ford appeared in an international against England at Roker Park. Despite scoring two goals Ford still ended up on the losing side. England ran out 4-2 winners.

Blackpool's Mudie miskicks his effort on goal and Hedley manages to clear in the League match at Bloomfield Road on 20 January 1951. Sunderland supporters always looked forward to visits to Blackpool to sample the non-football entertainment on offer (even in winter).

Sunderland's Billy Walsh and Brown of Blackpool challenge for the ball in the same match. Goals from Dickie Davis and Trevor Ford earned Sunderland a 2-2 draw against the Seasiders.

The one and only Len Shackleton. Sunderland broke the transfer record when they paid Newcastle £20,050 to bring his extraordinary talent to Roker Park in 1948. On Christmas Day 1940 Shackleton recorded the unusual feat of playing two matches for two different clubs. On the morning he played for Bradford Park Avenue against Leeds United at Elland Road. Then in the afternoon he turned out for Bradford City at Huddersfield. Wartime regulations allowed players to appear as guests for different clubs.

The 'Clown Prince of Soccer' in England shirt and cap. Only five full caps was poor reward for such a brilliant footballer. After making his debut against Denmark in a 0-0 draw in September 1948 Shack was on the winning side in every international appearance he made after. The last of these was a 3-1 victory over reigning World champions West Germany in December 1954.

Supporters who turned up at Roker Park for the FA Cup tie against Southampton on 27 January 1951 were greeted by the unusual sight of Sunderland turning out in black and white stripes. Because of a clash of colours the FA ruled that both teams had to change with Sunderland borrowing a set of strips from neighbours Newcastle.

Johnny Mapson beats Bates of Southampton to the ball in the Fourth Round tie. A brace of goals from Dickie Davis settled the issue. After beating Norwich in the next round Sunderland advanced into the quarter-finals. Wolves gained a 1-1 draw at Roker and then won the replay at Molineux 3-1.

Raich Carter leads out Hull City against the club where he first made his name. The teams met for the East Riding Invitation Trophy at Boothferry Park on 28 April 1952. This was played annually by Hull City who invited Sunderland to mark a very special occasion – Raich Carter's last game before retiring from football.

After the game most of the near 30,000 crowd gathered on the pitch in front of the grandstand. The man who had led Hull to the Third Division title and had helped save them from relegation was given a rapturous reception. The match itself had ended in a 2-2 draw, after the home side had been 2-0 up. Two goals from Trevor Ford in the last quarter of an hour levelled the score.

Because the teams had drawn the captains tossed a coin to see who would keep the trophy for the first six months. Fred Hall called correctly and the trophy's first port of call was Roker Park. Although billed as Raich Carter's last game it was to prove not to be so. In January 1953 he was lured out of retirement to play for Cork Athletic and helped them to win the FA of Ireland Cup.

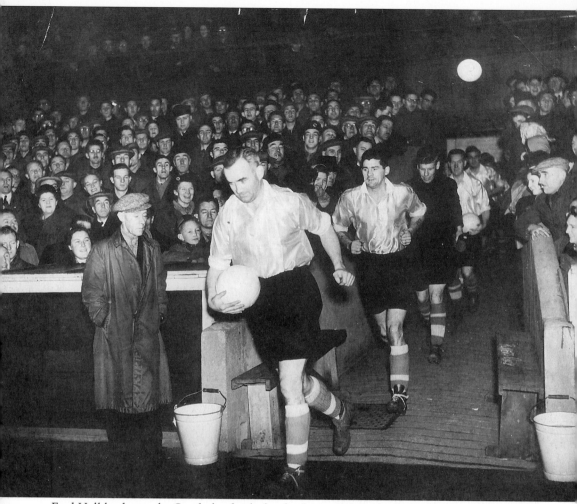

Fred Hall leads out the Sunderland side for the first match under Roker Park's new floodlights on 10 December 1952. Sunderland played in what were described as 'flame coloured luminous shirts'. The opposition for the occasion was provided by Dundee. The star of the visitor's team was Billy Steel who cost £23,000 (double the previous Scottish record) when bought from Derby County two years before. Steel had scored four goals in a match against Northern Ireland the previous month.

A crowd of 34,352 were treated to a great night of football with Sunderland eventually running out 5-3 victors. Although the cost of installing the 75 pylons and arc lamps ran into thousands of pounds the running costs were tiny in comparison with those of today. Sunderland paid no more than £1 for the electricity for the Dundee game in 1952. A spokesman for NEEB at the time said the floodlights used energy costing 7s 6d an hour. Club secretary George Crow commented, 'it was like a Technicolour film… I think we have got a real success here.' At the Football League annual meeting in the summer of 1955 Sunderland proposed that postponed matches should be played under floodlights. The proposal was adopted despite the fact many clubs at the time still did not have floodlights.

Welsh international Ray Daniel was a £27,000 signing from Arsenal in the 1953 close season. At the time Daniel said, 'I had nothing to do with deciding how much Sunderland would pay, but I will not be happy until Sunderland supporters are saying "He's worth every penny of it".' Whilst with the Gunners Daniel played for Wales against England at Roker Park in November 1950. During his stay at Sunderland he continued to be selected for his country and went on to win a total of 21 caps.

Tommy Wright gets down low to head for goal in a friendly against Third Lanark at Roker Park. Sunderland had paid the Scottish club £20,000 for the services of George Aitken in November 1951. Both Wright and Aitken won Scottish caps during their time at Roker.

Sunderland's programme for Bolton's League visit to Roker Park on Easter Monday 1953. Two goals from Tommy Wright gave Sunderland a 2-0 victory. This avenged a 5-0 defeat against Wanderers at Burnden Park on the Good Friday.

Tommy Wright's performances on the right wing, centre forward or inside forward earned him three caps for Scotland. In January 1955 he moved back north when he joined East Fife as part of the deal that brought Charlie Fleming to Roker. By coincidence Wright and Fleming had played together as youngsters for Fifeshire side Blairhall Colliery.

Tommy Wright in action against the famous gold and black of Wolverhampton Wanderers at Molineux. Wright enjoyed playing against Wolves: in six League meetings he scored four goals.

The Wolves 'keeper acrobatically saves from Tommy Wright at Roker Park. During the 1950s the Molineux club were one of the top sides in the country. Under inspirational skipper Billy Wright they won the championship three times during the decade. Fixtures between the clubs were so popular they were often arranged for the Christmas or New Year period.

Ray Daniel sends Manchester City 'keeper Savage the wrong way from the penalty spot in the match at Maine Road on 8 September 1956. The 62nd minute goal came too late as City were already 3-0 up and held on to the final whistle. The scoreline would have been even heavier if it had not been for Johnny Bollands' brilliant display in the Sunderland goal. One of City's goalscorers was Don Revie who was to join Sunderland only two months later.

Sunderland goalkeeper Johnny Bollands at full stretch. He faced stiff competition for the goalkeeper's jersey from Scottish international Willie Fraser. The result was that he was limited to sixty-one League appearances in a four year Roker career.

Ray Daniel gets in an effort on the Manchester United goal in the League meeting at Roker Park on 13 October 1956. Left to right: Duncan Edwards, Ted Purdon, Ray Daniel, Mark Jones, Bill Foulkes and Eddie Colman. United were the reigning League champions with an outstanding young team. Twenty-year-old Duncan Edwards was already a legend in the game having become the youngest player to win an England cap eighteen months before. A 3-1 win at Roker helped them retain the title but it turned out to be a poignant occasion as it was the last time the Busby Babes played at Sunderland. In February 1958 the plane carrying the United team back from a European Cup tie crashed on take-off. Eight United players were killed, including Edwards, Jones and Colman. Centre half Bill Foulkes survived and was in the team that won the European Cup at Wembley ten years later.

At the time of the Munich Air Disaster Ernie Taylor was due to join Sunderland from Blackpool. Because of United's dire straits the Sunderland directors allowed the little inside right to go to Old Trafford. At the end of 1958, once the immediate crisis was over, Taylor eventually joined his hometown club.

Six

More 'Downs' than 'Ups' 1958-73

Relegations then Cup Dream

Charlie Hurley was one of the greatest players ever to wear the famous red and white Sunderland shirt. Yet he could hardly have had a worse baptism to his Roker career. After 7-0 and 6-0 defeats at Blackpool and Burnley respectively, the young centre half must have wondered what he had let himself in for. For the next decade the brilliant performances turned in by 'King' Charlie made him a legend on Wearside.

Before the dangers of smoking were known football followers were targeted by tobacco companies. Various sets of football cards were given away in packets of cigarettes. In the post-war period the trend of cigarette cards switched to safer products like tea. In 1958 Lambert's of Norwich produced a series which included Sunderland. The badge showed the town's old coat of arms.

Tough tackling Jimmy McNab made his Sunderland debut as an eighteen-year-old against Ipswich on 20 September 1958. Shortly after the start of Sunderland's first season in the Second Division Alan Brown decided to put all his faith in a policy of youth. He pitched the former Scottish Schoolboy international into the first team along with Len Ashurst and Cecil Irwin. All three were to be seasoned veterans when promotion was eventually achieved.

After impressing scouts from a number of clubs while playing for St Hilda's School in Southwick, Jimmy Montgomery signed for his hometown club in October 1960. He made his debut a year later against Walsall in the League Cup while still only seventeen.

Ian Lawther challenges for the ball in the match against Lincoln City at Roker Park on 3 September 1960. At the time Lincoln were bottom of the Second Division with Sunderland hoping to mount a promotion challenge. Lawther had been the club's leading goalscorer the previous season and a goal against Lincoln helped towards him repeating the feat at the end of the 1960-61 campaign. The signing of Brian Clough in the summer of 1961 was to signal the end of the Northern Ireland international's Roker career.

Sunderland's Ambrose Fogarty looks on as the Lincoln 'keeper covers his goal. The game ended in a 2-2 draw with goals from Lawther and Fogarty. This was Sunderland's first dropped home point of the season and they eventually finished in 6th place.

Len Ashurst (left) and Brian Clough had Roker careers that contrasted sharply. Full back Ashurst made over 400 League appearances for the club between 1958 and 1970. Prolific goalscorer Clough played only 61 League games but scored 54 goals in his brief stay on Wearside. Both men went into management: Ashurst was Roker boss between 1984 and 1985, while Clough was Sunderland supporters' choice for the post for many years.

ENGLISH CUP - Sixth Round

Sunderland v. TOTTENHAM

AT ROKER PARK GROUND, SUNDERLAND,

ON SATURDAY, MARCH 4th - 1961

At 3-0 p.m.

GROUND   Fulwell End

N⁰ 3052

This Ticket is issued subject to the Rules and Regulations of the F. A. and the F.L. Price of Tickets will not be returnable in any circumstances if the match has to be abandoned or postponed.

PRICE 3/6

A ticket for Tottenham's Sixth Round FA Cup visit on 4 March 1961. Over sixty thousand packed into Roker Park to see if Sunderland could knock Spurs off their 'Double' chasing course.

When Willie McPheat scored an equaliser against the Cup favourites at Roker Park some of the ecstatic supporters spilled on to the pitch. Despite having played all over the world Danny Blanchflower had never heard anything like the 'Roker Roar' before. He and the rest of the Spurs team were thankful for the respite the mini invasion brought. It gave them time to compose themselves and they managed to withstand the Sunderland onslaught. In the replay at White Hart Lane, Spurs stormed into the next round with a 5-0 victory.

Skipper Charlie Hurley is carried shoulder high by team-mates after promotion was assured in the last home game of the 1963-64 season. To the relief of the 50,827 crowd a 2-1 win over Charlton booked a return to the First Division. After the game the players did a lap of honour before returning to the dressing-room. The crowd would not leave and started chanting 'Charlie, Char-lie'. The Sunderland skipper and the rest of the team were forced to come out again.

Before joining Sunderland in April 1961 George Herd had already played for Scotland five times. His transfer from Clyde cost the club £42,500. The skilful inside forward only missed 3 games in the promotion campaign scoring 13 goals.

Sunderland's line-up at the start of the 1964-65 season. Back row: Cecil Irwin, Martin Harvey, Derek Forster, Jimmy McNab, Len Ashurst. Front row: Brian Usher, George Herd, Nicky Sharkey, Charlie Hurley, Johnny Crossan, George Mulhall.

Fifteen-year-old Derek Forster made history when he played in Sunderland's first game back in the top flight on 22 August 1964. The England Schoolboys 'keeper became the youngest ever First Division player in the game against Leicester City at Roker. After three games the club brought in the experienced Sandy McLaughlan and then the consistency of Jimmy Montgomery, after returning from injury, restricted the young prodigy's progress.

Within days of Ian McColl's appointment as Sunderland manager Jim Baxter was signed for a record £72,500 fee from Rangers. The club had been chasing the stylish Scottish international even before McColl took over. His performances at Ibrox and for the national side had brought 'Slim Jim' to the attention of all the top clubs. On his arrival at Roker he remarked 'This is wonderful. I couldn't wish to be going to a better club'.

At the time George Kinnell signed for Sunderland in October 1966 he was Oldham's leading goalscorer, however, at Roker he was to make his mark in defence. The Scot made an impressive debut at centre half in a 2-1 victory over Stoke City. This ended a run of 9 League and Cup games without a win. The next game proved how valuable an acquisition Kinnell was when Sunderland recorded a 3-0 win at St James' Park.

Sunderland first team squad for the 1968-69 season. Back row: Geoff Butler, George Mulhall, Martin Harvey, Ian Porterfield, Colin Suggett, Len Ashurst. Middle row: Calvin Palmer, Billy Hughes, Jim Montgomery, Charlie Hurley, Bruce Stuckey. Front row: Bobby Kerr, Gordon Harris, George Kinnell, Colin Todd, Cecil Irwin, George Herd.

One of the greatest post-war Sunderland players was undoubtedly Colin Todd. Born in Chester-le-Street, he was already an outstanding talent when he joined the club as a fifteen-year-old in 1965. By the time he was twenty he was captaining the team in the First Division. In February 1971 Derby County paid £170,000, a record for a defender, for his services. His move to the Baseball Ground brought a belated England call up but 27 full caps was scant reward for this majestic footballer.

The Sunderland programme for the FA Cup Fourth Round tie against Peterborough on 18 February 1967. In the previous round Brentford had been beaten 5-2 and a crowd of almost 44,000 gathered to see if further progress could be made against the Posh. They were not to be disappointed: the Third Division side were thrashed 7-1. The next round brought three bone-crunching games with Leeds United. The first game at Roker ended 1-1 with Bobby Kerr suffering a broken leg after a tackle by Norman Hunter. The scoreline finished the same at Elland Road before a record crowd of 57,892. Sunderland finally went down 2-1 in a decider at Hull, finishing with only nine men after George Herd and George Mulhall had been sent off for protesting a penalty decision.

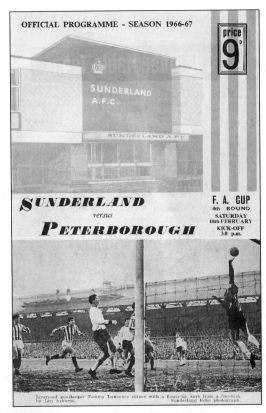

OFFICIAL PROGRAMME - SEASON 1966-67

price 9d

SUNDERLAND A.F.C.

SUNDERLAND
versus
PETERBOROUGH

F. A. CUP
4th ROUND
SATURDAY
18th FEBRUARY
KICK-OFF
3.0 p.m.

Liverpool goalkeeper Tommy Lawrence shines with a finger-tip save from a free-kick by Len Ashurst. Sunderland Echo photograph.

Hat-trick hero against Peterborough Neil Martin was one of Sunderland's finest post-war centre forwards. Having scored over a hundred goals in Scottish football with Hibernian Martin joined Sunderland in October 1965. By the time he moved on to Coventry City in 1968 he had scored a goal in almost every other game he played for Sunderland. He went on to become one of the few men to have scored a century of League goals in both England and Scotland.

Dave Watson soars above the Orient defence to get a header on goal. Bought from Rotherham for £100,000 in 1970 as a centre forward, he was switched to his original position of centre half and never looked back. After the Cup run brought him to national prominence he won his first England cap against Portugal at the age of 27. He went on to make a total of 65 appearances for his country whilst with five different clubs. After leaving Sunderland he won caps with Manchester City, Werder Bremen, Southampton and Stoke City.

Scottish Under 23 international Dick Malone signed for Sunderland from Ayr in 1970 and quickly became a favourite of the Roker crowd. His surging runs from right back supplemented his defensive prowess. All the newspaper talk before the 1973 Cup Final centred on the havoc Eddie Gray would wreek down the left flank. The Sunderland man silenced his doubters with a performance which forced Leeds to substitute the ineffective Gray. Three years after the Cup triumph he helped Sunderland to promotion to the top flight.

Billy Hughes was an important factor in the triumphant Cup run in 1973. Crucial goals in both games against Manchester City and in the semi-final allowed Sunderland to progress. A product of the club's successful youth system the young Scot's direct style made him a crowd favourite. Just after the 1973 Cup run got underway brother John the former Celtic favourite joined him at Roker. An injury in his first game against Millwall put an end to his Sunderland career. In 1975 Billy Hughes became the last Sunderland player to be capped for Scotland.

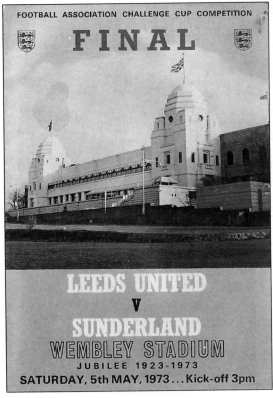

The 1973 FA Cup Final programme celebrating the Jubilee Wembley Final. There was a big difference in price from Sunderland's last Wembley appearance. Inflation had pushed the price from 6d (2½p) in 1937 to 15p in 1973: a six fold increase. Sunderland's ticket allocation had also increased since 1937 doubling to 20,000. However, this still left the Finalists with less than half of the total capacity.

123

Vic Halom comes away with the ball from Allan Clarke in the Final. Clarke was seen as a potential match winner but from the very first tackle Ritchie Pitt had his measure. For Leeds' captain Billy Bremner (left of picture) it was to be another question of so near yet so far. Although another trophy was denied them they did bounce back the following season to win the League.

The signing of Vic Halom from Luton Town for £35,000 in February 1973 was the final piece in Bob Stokoe's jigsaw. The bustling centre forward brought power to an attack that was now capable of scoring against any team in the land. Halom's thunderbolt against Manchester City in the Fifth Round replay was one of the greatest goals ever seen at Roker Park.

124

The moment that stunned the football world: Ian Porterfield hammers home the goal that brought the FA Cup back to Sunderland after a gap of thirty-six years. Unusually it was not scored with the Scot's cultured left foot but with his unfavoured right.

Sunderland's goal hero could have been playing on opposite sides in the 1973 Cup Final. As a schoolboy he spent time at Elland Road but was home sick and he did not return to Yorkshire. Leeds' loss was Sunderland's gain when he joined the club from Raith Rovers in 1967.

Jimmy Montgomery

With Leeds piling on the pressure in search of an equaliser Jimmy Montgomery produced one of the greatest saves ever seen at Wembley. He saved a goalbound Trevor Cherry header but the ball fell to Peter Lorimer. The man with the hardest shot in the game struck it perfectly. Monty flung himself at the ball and somehow managed to parry it away.

Apart from his wonder save at Wembley Monty's performances for the club during the 1960s and '70s make him a candidate for the title of Sunderland's greatest ever goalkeeper. After a spell on loan at Southampton Monty eventually joined Birmingham City in March 1977 after seventeen years at Roker.

The Sunderland skipper on the shoulders of his team-mates proudly holds the Cup aloft. Bobby Kerr had fought his way back from a twice broken leg to lead his side to Cup glory.

The Wembley heroes proudly display the FA Cup. Back row: Arthur Cox (coach), Vic Halom, Dick Malone, Jimmy Montgomery, Ritchie Pitt, Dave Watson, Bob Stokoe (manager). Front row: David Young, Ron Guthrie, Billy Hughes, Bobby Kerr, Dennis Tueart, Ian Porterfield, Mickey Horswill. Like their 1937 counterparts the victorious players received a tremendous welcome on their return to Wearside. The drive from Carrville to Roker Park was cheered by 500,000 people.